Into the Light
by
Gabriel Collins

Published on 1st March 2007 by

Tern Press Ltd
Dublin
Ireland

www.ternpress.com

Info@ternpress.com

ISBN 10 0-9554300-0-3
ISBN 13 978-0-9554300-0-8

Front Cover Siobhan Ryan

Editing John O'Brien

Dedicated to my wife and family

Foreword

Similes, metaphors, alliteration, onomatopoeia were all consigned to a time, when for me poetry and schoolbooks including the poems of Donne, Elliot, and Wordsworth were burned on a sacrilegious pyre along with Paradise Lost, the Wandering of Aengus and the meandering works of other lesser known poets.

The poetic memories were left in what seemed to be their rightful place, among the rows of wooden desks and squeaking chalk blackboards. So that was that, the end of formal education and dissecting and analysing poetry. Something learned, little understood and quickly forgotten.

So it stayed until a chance meeting with Seamus Heaney in a cellar in Krakow, a few pints of Guinness, a long night and a new understanding of how poetry comes from a fusion of the mind and soul.

Since that night in the cellar, poems have accompanied me on many a long journey. Endless waits in airports, traffic jams and time spent dining alone have been turned into moments of some pleasure, when an embryonic thought grew into something that resembled a poem.

"So more than Guinness flowed out of that Polish cellar … I'm glad the poems started to get a decent head on them" Seamus Heaney.

Then there followed the guide books extolling how to write the perfect verse, the dos and don'ts and the discovery of the obvious, that every poet has a unique style.

At this point, I met in London, William Meredith and Richard Harteis - and they provided insight into their work and offered some useful pointers.

Gabriel has "the sensitivity of a poet for sure - Of course, we all have deep emotions but the poet combines a facility with words and image to make a reader feel and see with a heightened appreciation. I like how the poems often turn at the end with their epiphanies." Richard Harteis with William Meredith

So thanks to the established masters, who despite their busy schedules took time out to offer support and guidance without which this volume would never come into the light.

"Into the Light" is a collection of poems on which light is played, reflected, refracted, diffracted to simplify shadows and reveal the subject from a changed perspective. The images compliment, strengthen, contrast, weaken or simply introduce confusion, leaving the reader to interpret in a unique and personal way.

I hope you enjoy.

Gabriel

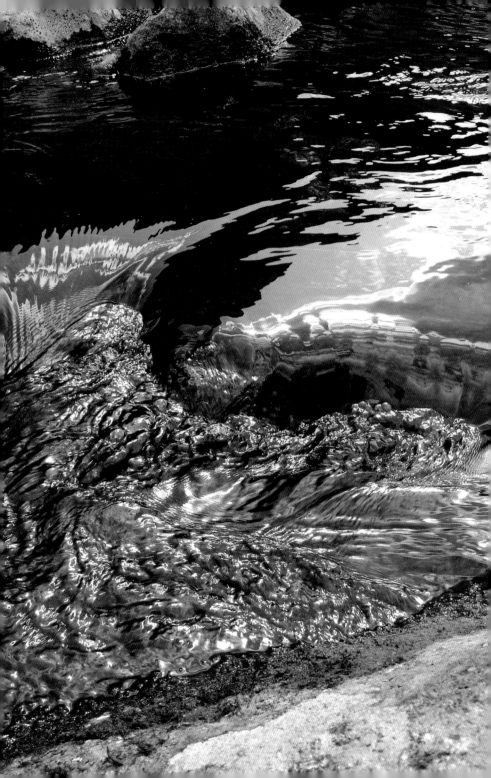

Contents

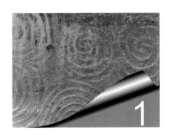

Romana

Closer to me, she's coming
Tall, long legs. Short skirt
Riding over tanned knees.
Black hair bouncing tumbles
Over bare shoulders.
Eyes dark, smiling.

Smiling, yes, at me, this woman.
This goddess
In a crowded room.
Coming closer to talk.
To talk to - me.

Standing close – she slightly
Bends – leaning towards me.
So close – her hand almost.
Almost touching me – her
Breathe so fresh.

Her voice, so clear, a little hint
Of Italy – as she speaks.
Are you ready? I hear her say.
Large number 7 Piazza Romana
- No onions.
I whisper in reply.

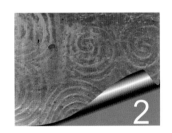

Dawn

A moment, a time,
To be with you
To call your name
And say I love you

Another day dawning
Silhouettes clearing,
Sky light brightening,
Garbage trucks cleaning
---- last nights debris.

As life's frozen cold,
Still seek seven dollars
For night sleep.
Yet still I seek.

A moment, a time,
To be with you
To call your name
And say I love you

Mind in haze, alcohol induced
Wander streets, party over
Empty streets.

Among life's debris
Drug enhanced
Bag carriers,

Doorway sleepers and
They who hang about.

Still I seek

A moment, a time,
To be with you
To call your name
And say I love you

As it dawns
I wonder
Can it ever be true?

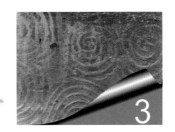

Orchestral Strings

Tunelessly, swaying, oscillating,
Cast against a steel grey winters sky
Pitching, rolling, moored on a rising tide,
Masts tall, slender, steel guys taut,
Vibrating like a discordant orchestra.

Awaiting springs return – the
Rush of the beat, sails straining
Keeling, - tacking running tuned
To winds and open seas.

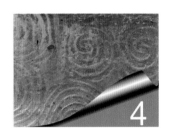

Two Moons

You walked among the trees
In the dead of night
Scarcely nothing to be seen
But your eyes beautiful and white.

Black and dark amongst the trees
Yet eyes clear like two full moons
You come and offer for sale
Not some local tourist junk.

Or mind bending narcotics
But your own sexy body
And for thirty euro pieces
You provide quite simple pleasure.

While sharing with the unwitting
Your deadly secret virus.

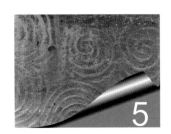

Can't Read

I can't read now, even can't see
But I know I am here.
I can't touch now, even can't feel.
But I know I am here
Ha, you say, what's the point?

I can't walk either, even can't stand
But that's not so bad, I am here
I can't sit either, even can't move
But it's not so bad, I am still here
Still you keep saying, you can't see the point.

I can't talk, ha, can't even mumble
Some would say that's good, silent at last,
But I don't mind, I am here.
I can't smell, not even my ass.
I bet you are saying that's just as well,
But who cares, I know I'm here
Ha I can still hear you, asking why bother.

You think that's bad, it gets worse
Kidneys, bowel, liver all the googey bits going
But I don't care, cause I'm here.

It's me, I dream of the stars, the sun
The rivers and fields, the friends once had
The loves, the joys, the kids, so much
So much to think and that's me.

Now more morphine, to kill the pain
Now that's bad, and I really care
As I get confused and forget it's me here.

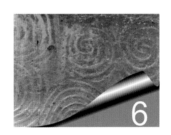

Moment of Recognition

You glanced
And in a micro moment,
I caught your slight smile,
Rising almost imperceptibly
From your lips to eyes.

And in that time,
I returned a smile,
As if reflected from a mirror
Or by some auto thought.

You walked past.
I continued – on.

Four more steps,
Cerebral thoughts
Commenced – I turned.

As if drawn, by
An unseen string
You stopped, head
And shoulders slowly
Turned – until

We stood on the pavement.
Those seven paces of separation
Almost like a chasm.

Then you being the braver
Of the two – stepped forward.
Standing within touching space
You spoke and your welcome
Words ran round my head.

As I stood almost entranced,
Like Alexandra smitten by Venus
And I by your eyes,
Of every deepening blue.

I heard you talk.

Words like –, Long –, Time
How –, and –, Being,
Reached some inner sensors.

From me – only silence.

But then I heard a disembodied
Voice, like a base drum
Or the low tone Bell of Big Ben
Say I think you are mistaken.

Your eyes changed – a quick
Blink and I heard you murmur.

And in the instant, as you
Turned - away – your smile
Dissipated, – your pale
Complexion, – filled by rising
Tide of embarrassment,
Like a chameleon changing,
From winter pale to sun burnt red.

And I walked on.
Knowing who had spoken.
Recognising the fool within.

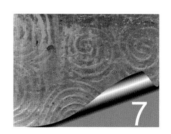

Painted Words

The poet's easel is the table
His canvas the notepad
His brush the pencils and pens
And his paint – the thoughts
And words.

Each carefully crafted, shaped
Coloured, structured till they
- fill the page,
Giving form to more than
Strung out words but an image
Painted in words and ink which
Draws one into its core.

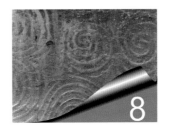

My First Time

Perspiring, beads of sweat,
Glistening on forehead, rivulets
Forming irregular, meandering lines
Streaming down face, curving round neck
To back and soaking sheet.

Lying in bed, she's covered lightly
Legs outstretched, spread wide
Breasts heavy, back arching
Grasping for hand – fingers in fingers
Entwined – vice like.

Deep inside, so tight
Almost crushed, when
I move she screams
So loud – uncaring
But what will the neighbours say
Fuck the neighbours
            --- I've waited so long.

As she screams, I'm coming closer
Disjointed voices urging
"Push", "squeeze" "harder" "hold me".

Moving faster
        - eyes closed
Nearly there – covered in wet yucky mess
Is there no better way?

She's calmed, almost relaxed
I wait quietly, sensing, unmoving,

Waiting.

Waiting for the tension to rebuild.

Her muscles quiver, shake, vibrate
Pulsing through me – I wait
Know it's now --- one long last
Scream, squeeze, push

And

I come

Exhausted.

Into the light.

A once in a lifetime experience,
Never to be repeated.
Hey, get the rest of me out and let
My life begin.

Thanks Ma.

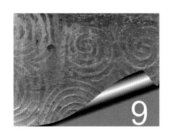

Light

Night turns into dawn,
Darkness retreats,
The early morning light,
Like a photographer
Turns black into shapes
Unravelling the forms
Then reveals
Intimate details.

So to with people
Thoughts, secrets
Desires and needs
Are revealed as friendship
Grows and the darker
Shadows retreat.

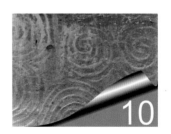

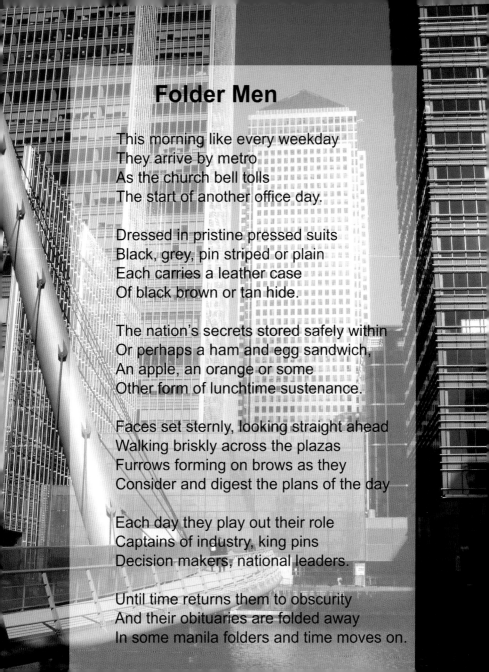

Folder Men

This morning like every weekday
They arrive by metro
As the church bell tolls
The start of another office day.

Dressed in pristine pressed suits
Black, grey, pin striped or plain
Each carries a leather case
Of black brown or tan hide.

The nation's secrets stored safely within
Or perhaps a ham and egg sandwich,
An apple, an orange or some
Other form of lunchtime sustenance.

Faces set sternly, looking straight ahead
Walking briskly across the plazas
Furrows forming on brows as they
Consider and digest the plans of the day

Each day they play out their role
Captains of industry, king pins
Decision makers, national leaders.

Until time returns them to obscurity
And their obituaries are folded away
In some manila folders and time moves on.

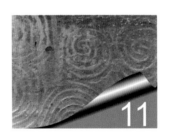

The night without stars

We strolled along the beach
In the early morning glow
Side by side we thread through
Lives of fifty million years ago

Now pounded into particles
Each a story on its own
-        the life of a starfish
-        the shape of a mollusc
Or some ancient crustacean
Long lost to our time.

Our fifty years is nothing more
Than a grain within this sand
And yet we spent the night reliving.
Our story told, retold, shaped
And revised as another beer
Against the rhythmic and the half beat
Of some invasive music
Improved the telling.

Yet in the night without stars
As we were brought to earth
One star shone – rose high
And showed another way.

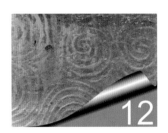

Pic Nic

Orange-red rug spread out in a sea
Of daisies white, yellow dandelions
Peeping through early summer grass.

Clear skies, blue overhead
Sun filled warmth on back and neck
Buttons undone – sleeves loose
Sitting so close, side by side,
Arms intertwined.

Red wine uncorked, bread rolls
Stuffed with Harrods best open
Set among olives, salami, cheese
Lunch ready, reaching out,
Fingers touch electric.

Glass clinks – relax, laugh
Smile, joke, time forgotten
Talk of times past, life other
Loves and hopes.

Sun dipping past, pale green
Chestnut leaves, creeping shadow
Late afternoon – heat cooling
Feelings high, buttons up.
They go. To where?

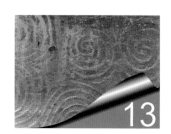

Kathy Says

Time spent
In rain, downpour and drizzle
Time spent with you,
Wet.

But did I care
Did I feel the rain?

Did I feel my shirt?
Transparent, so wet,
Revealing
My navel and breasts
Clinging like film.

But did I care.
Did I feel the rain?

Soaking my hair
Rolling down face
Undoing my work

But did I care

As I stood there
Eyes to eyes
Lips on lips
Body to body
Feeling nothing
But you.
And I sure cared.

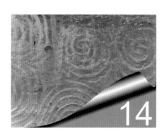

My Love

I fell in love so young
Hardly more than a kid
Spotty faced, post puberty
But just fourteen
When I felt your soft touch
On my lips – your breath
Warm in my mouth.

My body trembled in anticipation
I felt the rush of blood to my head
And the excitement of having you
Again and again –
And when it was over
You left me calm and relaxed.

There were times – many times
When I couldn't wait for you
I needed you, needed you now.
My desires went out of control
As I stole off to the bedroom
And my lust was fulfilled.

As an adolescent we often
Did it secretly, in hidden places
Afraid of being caught, being seen,
I had you in the hay shed
        behind the school
                even in the loo
Anywhere to be with you.

As I grew older, I walked with you
Along the beach in the early morning
The fresh sea air on my face
As I held you in my hand.
At these moments,
You were my heaven.

But it wasn't all plain sailing
We had our moments
Many a time I said stop
No more – I can live without you
I don't need you any more
Our friendship has grown stale.

But as often as I said No,
I said just one more time,
I need to feel you touch my lips,
Your breath deep in my mouth.
The tingle on my tongue.
And the desire reaching out from
My belly, rushing through my blood,
As you make me feel in a way
No other could.

Time came and went and
You were still my love.
And then they said hey
No more – what a dirty thing
You're worse than a whore.

But I fought off all the be grudgers
The ner do wells, the alarmists
And the meds.

I had known you so long.
You were such a part of me.
My life without you would
Be so empty, depressing, shallow.

And then they treated us like
Lepers – no more they said.
Confine your dirty pleasures
To your home.

Keep your filthy habits to yourself
Don't corrupt our kids,
Defile our homes and pubs

Drink our beers you may,
Enjoy the music and the craic,
But don't bring your dirty friend
And keep the smoke outside.

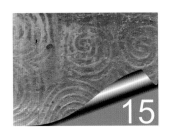

No Flowers

No flowers the notice reads
Of course no need.
Your journey was
And will always be
Lined with beautiful
Wild flowers.

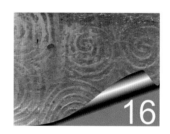

16

Adam

It's not hard to see why, they thought Adam was nobody.
Walk he couldn't and his hands were no use.
When he spoke dribbles flowed and moans gurgled out.

But he could press the right buttons to reverse or fast forward
His motorised chair with such precision and deftness
Only a well thinking brain could work out.

Yet drinking tea from a plastic cup held by caring hands
Or mushy food on a spoon pressed gently to his lips.
Must have been like a gourmet meal for he laughed.

And then smiled as he looked into the eyes
Of the caring young woman who saw
Beyond the wreck.
A somebody,
Struggling,
Maybe like her but in so different ways.

Then after the meal, her break now past,
She returned to her task
Feeding burgers and chips to the ever-growing mass,
In this Institution of institutions long slated and bemoaned.

Anger

When consumed with anger
My lips trembled, my face ashened.
My heart pounded, my head ached
And my words – those spirited words
That would prove I was right and would
Vindicate my position – came out.

Came out
With such anger and venom
That my argument was lost – before
They reached your ears.

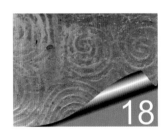

Chrysalis

Swaying, dithering in summer breeze
Pitched back and forth in raging storms.
Cocooned in downy white silken thread
Evolving – changing from the past
Fearing what you might become
Seeking the courage to self believe.

Then suddenly without though
The cocoon shell cracks – a slight
Jagged line meanders end to end.
Widens until the casement parts
And you
-          are left exposed
-          unprotected
Your future is now.

You unfurl – cast the tensions aside.
See yourself as you truly are.
A beautiful, sensitive, awe-inspiring
Creature – exuding desire and sensuality.
With newfound confidence you fly above the past.

To scent filled meadows – feeding on fragrant nectar
Rising on up draughts, weaving, threading, flittering
Iridescent in the afternoon sun as you live the life
Of dreams and dance the courtship dance of
-          summer butterflies.

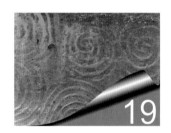

Soul Mate

Of course – from the outside, you looked pretty,
Attractive and all sexed up.
No one could imagine you, in my mother's words
Left on the shelf.

Within, you held greater depths
Mysterious, sensuous - at times
Bordering between exotic and erotic.

From the moment of first glance
I wanted – No – needed to know you.
Not just fleetingly.

But your every secret
That which makes you appealing
To men and indeed to women.

Yes women are drawn to you
And may even see a side
Which I – in my eagerness and
Desire to rush forward – missed.

I have travelled with you
Ate with you, slept with you
You have kept me awake thinking
And wondering where truth lay.

As I became more absorbed with you
Time passed in the world outside.
And now that it has come to The End
I know I won't give you up.
But keep you close
Longing to explore you again.

The day will come
When your words have faded
And I open you one more time
On Chapter One

The Dune

Whipped, swirling,
Wind borne, flecks of mica
Grains of stone, carried
Blindly in ragging storm.

Over dry, desolate landscape
Dunes, shifting, enlarging
Ever changing, shaped by wind
Direction and erosion.

Wind eases. A tiny grain
Its flight path changed, seemingly
Floats or drifts aimlessly
Down – followed by another
And yet more – until a
Small shape forms.

Then slowly as grain upon grain
Joins and settles a growing
Mound is formed
With time, it shape becomes
Distinguishable – putting a
Transitory mark on the landscape.

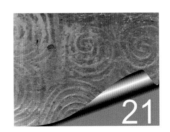

The Wall

After dark, pubs closing.
Lined up facing wall
Men stand
      legs parted
Shoulders stooped, maybe hunched
Trousers creased, shuffle in pocket.

Hands in front
      Waist high
Move about – unseen, secret work
Waiting – then it happens
Almost flows
-     unseen satisfaction.

Then quick trouser adjustment
Zip closing or button fastening
Pat on pocket
Step to left, straighten up
Feeling good
     Wallet filled
     With fresh new notes.

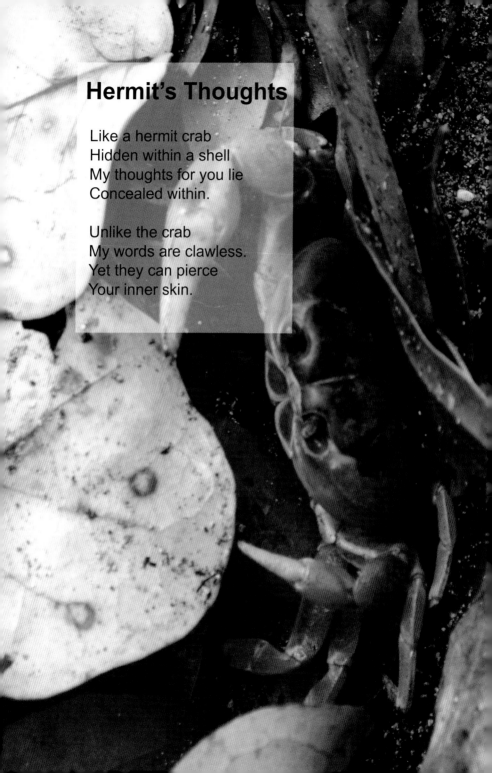

Hermit's Thoughts

Like a hermit crab
Hidden within a shell
My thoughts for you lie
Concealed within.

Unlike the crab
My words are clawless.
Yet they can pierce
Your inner skin.

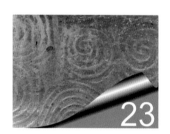

In Love

Wooden benches, straight lined,
They sit, watching and maybe wait.
Sunday best dressed, clean pants
Jacket neatly pressed over mam's
Ironed shirt.

Looks like home, feels like home
Same beers, same music
No rhythm and blues
No rock and roll
Same chat – "who won the match"
"Did you see the cut of Murphy"

Interspersed with fleeting glances
Across the bar – a keen eye on the locals.
"God doesn't she look great – very
Sexy – wouldn't mind a bit of that"

More beers raised and drowned.

Blonde hair, red top, tight pants.
They look and stare – sharing
Intimate thoughts – safely watching.

Wishing for more – afraid of no
They sit and sip and stay in love
With their safe dark beer.

Just

Just to feel you, to touch you
To see you, to hear you,
Is all I have to say.

Just want to feel you
To hold you
And be by your side.

Just want to hear you
Be near you
As you whisper I love you.

Just to feel you, to touch you
To see you, to hear you,
Is all I have to say.

Just want to see you
To touch you
As I look into your eyes

Just want to tell you
I love you
When you
Are not surprised.

Just to feel you, to touch you
To see you, to hear you,
Is all I have to say.

Tick of the Clock

Stillness, the quiet time before
Morning rush.
Like a silence, deafening in its
Intensity, enveloping all surrounds
Scarcely broken by
Periodic tick of the battery clock.

He sits at table
Elbow resting on wooden top
Face cradled in hand
Pondering, finger circling
Half circling, forming
Invisible letters on polished top.

He glances at clock, seven fifteen.

Head in hand, clock ticks
The silence away
Time changes
The sound of happy kids
Friendly banter into dead
And empty numbing silence

Finger absently, scribing
Letters, names, characters
He looks vacantly at the
Invisible names of the kids
Recalls the times so good,
The joy, the happiness.

Now the only sound of life
The constant tick of time
Passing second by arduous second.
Seven sixteen, the start of another quiet
Lifeless day.

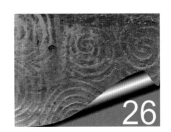

26

Toni

Today I saw where you rest
Beneath a summer garden
Under the Petunias, Begonias
Your toys – rattlers, bouncymen
Wooden train still look new
Your plastic windmill blowing
In a gentle breeze.

You left this world after a single year
A time spent in pain.
Gone before experiencing its
Pleasure, joys and knew the love.
Gone before you became known to us
But still loved by a few

Now fifteen years on, you're loved
As you were then by the minder of
This grave.

Universe

Confusing to scientists
Incompressible to me
The Universe is expanding
And growing with time.

But simpler and clearer
And easier to see
My universe is growing
In never ending time.

The moment the sperm
Penetrated the egg,
My universe spread
Out living it's womb.

Now I can
See, Hear, Speak
Read, Write, Fight
Love, Cry, Laugh.

I hope you agree
Not insignificant tasks
And there are more
But too many to mention.

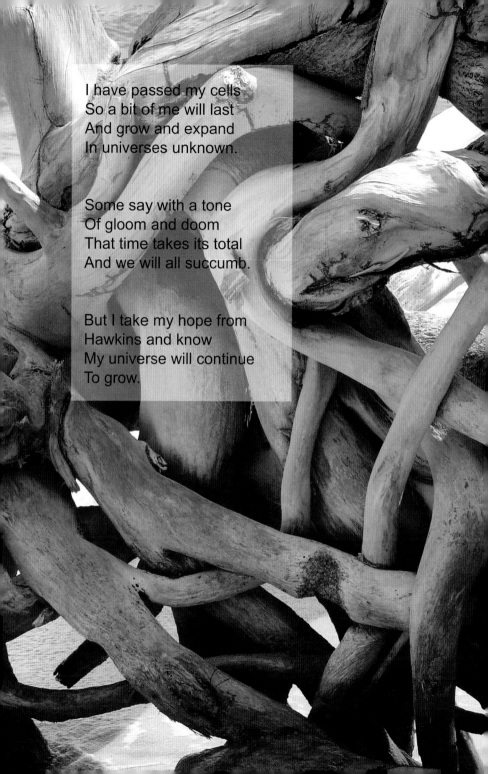

I have passed my cells
So a bit of me will last
And grow and expand
In universes unknown.

Some say with a tone
Of gloom and doom
That time takes its total
And we will all succumb.

But I take my hope from
Hawkins and know
My universe will continue
To grow.

Terror is

Hand, so small, shielding desert sun
Dark brown eyes, with that
Look of fear – a child's face
Grown old with thoughts of hate
Hugging Kalashnikov
Playing childhood games for real.

We call them terrorists
Rather than terror is
Depriving life, dignity, humanity.

29

Too Young

He wore a white bandana
With some indecipherable writing
Words we couldn't read
Or even understand.

Yet the pain and anguish
Were clearly written in his
Dark brown six year old eyes
As he contemplated the death
Of his sister by western might.

But he's too young to wonder
Why we will call him terrorist.

Year End

Beyond the twenty first, day starting to stretch
Sun moves slowly towards its zenith
Leaving a year, that's well worn
Having seen its character shaped, turned
Formed and changed and now almost
Scrubbed clean as it starts a fresh on the next
Annual pilgrimage through time.

What events await - what dreams to unfold?
What pleasures lie, tantalisingly close
Awaiting experience?
What lies ahead to be discovered?

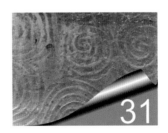

Acknowledgments

Without whom this Volume would have been very different or non existent.

Thanks to

Jenny Caldas

Bogota
Columbia

For her illustrations Falling and Illusionary used in the poem
"My Love" Copyright © Jenny Caldas

Jenny is an architect and her real passion is her art.
Her goal is to apply her love for art to her architectural work.

Thanks to

Daire

For his help and for the images "Soul Mate" and "Water"
Copyright © Daire

Also thanks to

BARA
British Association for Regional Art

Thanks to Seamus Heaney, Richard Harteis and William Meredith

Richard Harteis

Is the author of ten books of poetry and prose.
As well as a memoir entitled MARATHON published by W.W. Norton in 1989 to critical acclaim.

William Meredith

Poet Laureate of the United Sates, Library of Congress: The twenty-fifth poet to hold this position since its creation in 1936

Guggenheim Fellowship: Awarded in 1975 and 1976. Its purpose is to recognize men and women of high intellectual and personal qualifications who have already demonstrated an exceptional capacity for productive scholarship or exceptional creative ability in the arts.

The Pulitzer Prize: Awarded March 31, 1988 for Partial Accounts, this award recognises outstanding performance in journalism, letters, music, and drama.

The National Book Award: Meredith received this award in 1997 for Effort at Speech. The National Book Awards honour American books of the highest literary merit, books which have earned a permanent place in world literature.

Seamus Heaney

.

Nobel Prize - In 1995 he was awarded the Nobel Prize in Literature for what the Nobel committee described as "works of lyrical beauty and ethical depth, which exalt everyday miracles and the living past".

Whitbread Prize In 1996 his collection, The Spirit Level was published and won The Whitbread Book of the Year Award

Whitbread Prize In 1999 he again won The Whitbread Book of the Year Award for his re-translation of the epic Beowulf.

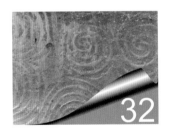

Publisher's Note

Thanks for purchasing this book, we hope you enjoyed the images and poems.

Gabriel will be interested in any feedback, comments or suggestions.
He can be contacted by email Gabriel@ternpress.com

He has read both formally and informally in Ireland, UK, USA and Australia and is always interested in hearing from Poetry societies, book clubs or reading groups.